Made in the USA
Columbia, SC
26 March 2025

55704378R00057